WE THE PEOPLE

The Statue of Liberty

by Ann Heinrichs

Content Adviser: Professor Sherry L. Field,
Department of Social Science Education, College of Education,
The University of Georgia

Reading Adviser: Dr. Linda D. Labbo,
Department of Reading Education, College of Education,
The University of Georgia

 COMPASS POINT BOOKS

Minneapolis, Minnesota

Compass Point Books
3722 West 50th Street, #115
Minneapolis, MN 55410

Visit Compass Point Books on the Internet at *www.compasspointbooks.com* or e-mail your request
to *custserv@compasspointbooks.com*

Editors: E. Russell Primm and Emily J. Dolbear
Photo Researcher: Svetlana Zhurkina
Photo Selector: Linda S. Koutris
Designer: Bradfordesign, Inc.

Library of Congress Cataloging-in-Publication Data

Heinrichs, Ann.
  The Statue of Liberty / by Ann Heinrichs.
    p. cm. —   (We the people)
  Includes bibliographical references and index.
  ISBN 0-7565-0100-8 (lib. bdg.)
    1. Statue of Liberty (New York, N.Y.)—Juvenile literature. 2. New York (N.Y.)—Buildings,
structures, etc.—Juvenile literature. 3. United States—Emigration and immigration—History—
Juvenile literature. [1. Statue of Liberty (New York, N.Y.) 2. National monuments. 3. Statues.
4. United States—Emigration and immigration—History.] I. Title. II. We the people (Compass
Point Books)
    F128.64.L6 H45 2001
    974.7'1—dc21   00-011018

TABLE OF CONTENTS

"WHAT A BEAUTIFUL SIGHT!"

"It was my birthday. I was thirteen years old that morning, and the first thing I saw was the Statue of Liberty. What a beautiful sight!"

Those were the words of a young girl from Eastern Europe. She and hundreds of others had spent weeks on a steamship crossing the Atlantic Ocean. Each person was full of hopes and dreams. Then they saw the Statue of Liberty in the sunlight and knew their journey was almost over.

The Statue of Liberty is one of the tallest statues in the world. It is the figure of a woman wearing robes and holding a torch. Many people call the statue Lady Liberty. It stands on Liberty Island in New York Harbor. For more than 100 years, its torch has welcomed people to America.

4

A dramatic view of the Statue of Liberty

5

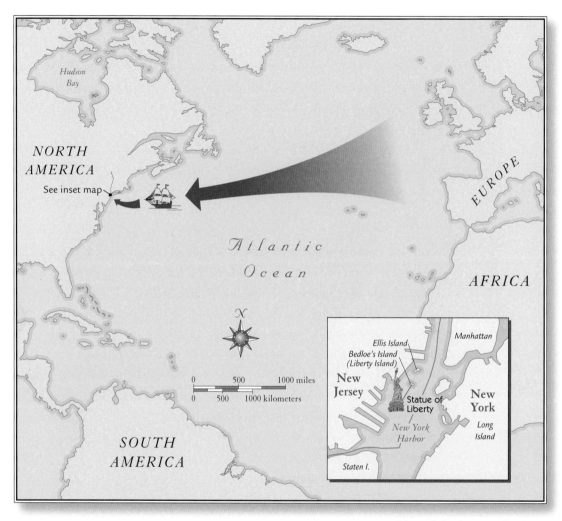

Map of the Statue of Liberty

Lady Liberty has greeted millions of newcomers. Their ocean journeys were not always easy.
But nearly everyone agreed that his or her arrival

made it worth all the pain. For many **immigrants**, life in America promised freedom, safety, and a better way of life. Just seeing the Statue of Liberty brought tears to their eyes. Feelings about the statue are just as strong today. It stands as a symbol of freedom to people around the world.

An immigrant family looks at the statue.

HOW IT ALL BEGAN

The Statue of Liberty was a gift from the people of France. But why would French citizens give thousands of dollars to build a statue in America? It was a gift of friendship. It honored the dream of freedom shared by people of both nations.

On July 4, 1776, the American colonists issued the Declaration of Independence. They were not happy under British rule. They wanted to be free. The colonists fought the American Revolution to win their freedom.

The French people felt a bond with the colonists. They sent troops to help the Americans fight the war. The United States won its freedom in 1783, and the French were overjoyed.

The signing of the Declaration of Independence

9

Frédéric-Auguste Bartholdi

As 1876 neared, some French people began to feel it was a time to celebrate. That year would mark the 100th **anniversary** of the Declaration of Independence. Soon the idea of a gigantic statue came up. It could be a birthday gift from France to the United States. A young sculptor named Frédéric-Auguste Bartholdi was chosen to build it.

Bartholdi began his great adventure by touring the United States in 1871. He was excited about the idea of the statue, and he knew just where it belonged. He sailed into New York Harbor and passed an island called Bedloe's Island. He could already imagine the statue standing on that island. And it would hold a torch high in the sky. It would represent the light of freedom shining for all.

Bartholdi met with many wealthy and powerful people during his trip to the United States. He spoke to everyone about the great statue that would honor the friendship between France and the United States. Many Americans were impressed with the plan. But few wanted to help pay for it. The French would have to begin on their own.

BUILDING THE STATUE

Back in France, Bartholdi started to work. First he made a model. It was one-fourth the planned size of the statue. Then the building began.

The statue was divided into 300 sections, and each part was built separately. People were amazed at the statue's size. Lady Liberty's thumb was as tall as a grown man. Her thumbnail was more than 1 foot (30 centimeters) long!

Parts of the Statue of Liberty under construction in Bartholdi's workshop

Such a huge statue needed a "skeleton." This would be a strong frame inside the statue to carry its weight. And it would have to stand up to the force of violent Atlantic storms. Bartholdi chose his friend Gustave Eiffel to design the framework. Eiffel was a brilliant engineer. He later became famous for building the Eiffel Tower in Paris, France.

Gustave Eiffel

Frédéric-Auguste Bartholdi used copper to make the statue's "skin," or outer shell. Workers hammered 452 sheets of copper into place. They

13

The framework of the statue being built in France

closely followed the flowing lines and curves of the

gigantic lady.

July 4, 1876, was the target date for finishing

the statue. But work was delayed again and again

because of a lack of money. Only the statue's right arm holding the torch was completed for the **centennial**. Bartholdi shipped this to the United States for a celebration in Philadelphia, Pennsylvania. There, for fifty cents, people could climb up a ladder inside the arm to a balcony.

The right hand and the torch of the Statue of Liberty were displayed at the 1876 Centennial Exhibition in Philadelphia.

LIBERTY ENLIGHTENING THE WORLD

Lady Liberty was finally finished in June 1884. Bartholdi named her "Liberty **Enlightening** the World." She stood 151 feet, 1 inch (46 meters) high. Her right hand held the torch. Her left arm held a tablet with the date of the Declaration of Independence—July 4, 1776—in Roman numerals.

A close-up view of the tablet in the Statue of Liberty's left hand

Her crown had seven spikes that stood for Earth's seven continents and seven seas. And under her

16

feet were broken chains. They represented the chains of slavery crushed beneath the feet of Liberty.

There was a problem back in the United States, however. Lady Liberty couldn't stand on the ground. She was so heavy that she would sink. The statue weighed 225 tons!

Richard Morris Hunt

It was America's job to build a **pedestal**—a sturdy stone base for the statue. U.S. architect Richard Morris Hunt began the pedestal. But Americans were not as excited about the project as the French were. Money for the pedestal ran out in seven months.

17

Joseph Pulitzer

Joseph Pulitzer owned the *New York World* newspaper. He thought that this lack of money was a shame. He himself was an immigrant from Hungary, and he valued his freedom. He begged in his newspaper for people to send in **donations**. And they did!

Some people could afford only a few pennies. Others sent nickels or dimes. But Pulitzer published the name of every single person who gave. Thanks to him and to hundreds of other Americans, the granite pedestal was finally finished. It would almost double the statue's height.

Now, the statue had to be shipped to the

18

Workers assembling the base of the Statue of Liberty

United States. It was taken apart in 350 pieces. The pieces were packed in wooden crates and then loaded onto the French ship *Isère*. What a bumpy ride the statue had! The ship almost turned over during one terrible storm at sea. But the statue

The French ship Isère sailing into New York Harbor

arrived safely. Workers put it back together one
piece at a time.

Americans couldn't wait to see their famous
gift. October 28, 1886, was set for the statue's day
of **dedication**.

20

DEDICATION DAY

The rain poured down that day. But more than a million people lined the streets of New York City for the big parade. And the harbor was filled with boats. President Grover Cleveland and other officials watched from a reviewing stand. They waved a proud salute to the rain-soaked marchers.

U.S. President Grover Cleveland arrives at Liberty Island for the dedication of the statue.

21

All New York celebrated throughout the day and night of the statue's dedication.

No one on the reviewing stand was more excited than the sculptor Frédéric-Auguste Bartholdi. He had dreamed of this day for more than twenty years.

President Cleveland and his team took off for

Bedloe's Island that afternoon. The island was now called Liberty Island. Lady Liberty stood there covered in heavy cloth.

Cleveland gave a fine speech, saying, "We will not forget that Liberty has made here her home. . . . [A] stream of light shall pierce the darkness of ignorance and man's oppression until Liberty enlightens the world." The French minister followed with a glorious speech of his own.

Meanwhile, Bartholdi was climbing up the long stairway inside the statue. A French flag covered its face. Bartholdi was supposed to pull the rope that would lower the flag. Somehow, in the middle of a speech, the flag dropped away. The crowd could see the lady's face and head. Forget the speakers! The people broke into a wild cheer that could be heard for miles.

THE IMMIGRANTS' JOURNEY

Millions of immigrants sailed to U.S. shores in the late 1800s. Now the Statue of Liberty welcomed them all. It stood for the promise of a new life of freedom. But it wasn't easy to reach that new life.

An immigrant's journey to America started long before he left his home. Some families sent just one member to America first. It was usually the father or the oldest son. That family member

The Statue of Liberty in 1894 as newly arriving immigrants would have seen it

24

worked hard and saved enough money to bring another family member over. It often took years before the whole family was together again.

The first step was to get to a seaport city. Some people took trains. Others rode on the family donkey. Some even walked. Then they waited to get official papers allowing them to leave. At last, they boarded a great steamship bound for America.

Passengers who could afford first-class or second-class tickets spent the trip in rooms above deck. But most immigrants were poor. They were steerage passengers. The steerage area was a deep, dark place inside the ship. It would be their home for as long as it took to cross the Atlantic Ocean. It could take anywhere from ten days to a month.

First- and second-class immigrants preparing to leave Europe

Conditions in steerage were awful. Iron pipes divided the area into bunk beds. Each person's space was about 6 feet (2 meters) long by 2 feet (60 centimeters) high. Steerage passengers breathed in dirt from the smokestacks and fumes from the engines. No one could take a bath. Many people got seasick and threw up constantly. The toilets were not built to handle so many people. The smell was horrible.

Some steerage passengers spent the voyage in a daze. They hardly ate. They just lay in their bunks waiting for it all to end. Others tried to keep

Most immigrants had an uncomfortable trip to the United States.

An aerial view of a ship sailing in New York Harbor near the statue

their spirits up. They sang, danced, played cards, and told tales of the wonderful life that lay ahead.

Then one day, someone let out an excited shout. The Statue of Liberty was in sight! One immigrant remembers that the trip was "the roughest thing I ever went through in my life. But when I saw that Statue of Liberty, I could have gone up to kiss it."

ISLAND OF HOPE, ISLAND OF TEARS

At last the ship docked in New York Harbor. First- and second-class passengers stepped ashore. But the steerage passengers still had a long way to go. They boarded a ferry for Ellis Island. There they entered a huge brick building.

Ellis Island

Ellis Island opened as the U.S. immigration center in 1892. Ellis Island was the Island of Hope for many. They would be free to follow their dreams once they left it.

Immigrants climbed a long stairway inside the main building. They carried their bags, bundles, and babies. As many as 5,000 passengers might arrive in one day. They often stood in line for hours. Then the examinations began.

First came the medical exams. Doctors checked everyone for eye infections, skin infections, heart disease, and a long list of other problems. Next came the "twenty-nine questions."

"Do you have any money? Who paid for your trip? Can you read and write? What kind of work do you do? Do you know anyone to stay with in the United States?"

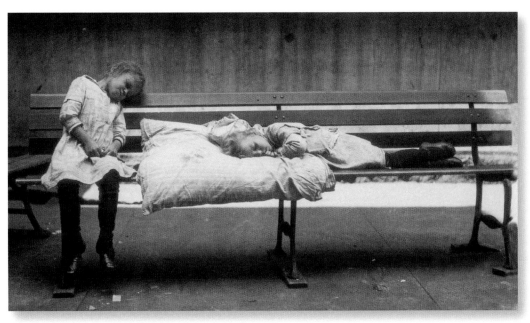

The journey to America could be exhausting.

wall of the statue's pedestal. The final lines are
often quoted:

> *Give me your tired, your poor,*
>
> *Your huddled masses yearning to breathe free,*
>
> *The wretched refuse of your teeming shore.*
>
> *Send these, the homeless, tempest-tost to me,*
>
> *I lift my lamp beside the golden door!*

A Nation of Immigrants

Why did so many people leave their homelands to come to the United States?

Before 1896, most immigrants came from northwestern Europe. Many were poor farmers from England, Scotland, and Ireland. Others came from Germany and the Scandinavian countries of Norway and Sweden. These countries had less and less farmland because their towns and cities were growing quickly.

In some places, crops failed and many people starved to death. Ireland's potato crops failed in the 1840s. Many people died of starvation. About 1.5 million Irish people came to the United States.

After 1896, most immigrants came from southern and eastern Europe. They included

Eastern Europeans fleeing brutal treatment in Poland and other countries

Italians, Slavs, and Russian and Polish Jews. European wars drove thousands of people to America. And in the 1880s, Russia and Poland began treating Jewish people brutally. More than 2 million Jews escaped to the United States.

These were just a few of the immigrant groups who found a better life in the United States. They made life richer for everyone by sharing their culture and skills. Immigrants built up the country's businesses. They made their music and art a part of American life. Together, they built the United States into the richest, most powerful nation in the world.

A NEW FACE FOR LADY LIBERTY

As time passed, the salty sea air rusted Lady Liberty's iron skeleton and copper skin. Storms drove saltwater into every crack. High winds loosened the joints. There was no avoiding the fact that Lady Liberty badly needed repairs.

Salty air and strong winds eventually took their toll on the statue.

The statue would be 100 years old in 1986. Repairs began in 1984. The ribs that link the skin to the frame were replaced with new ones made of stainless steel. Several hundred workers took the ferry to Liberty Island every day to repair the statue.

The United States celebrated the statue's rededication in 1986.

Among the workers was a team of French crafts workers. They came to build a new torch for the statue. It would be exactly like the one Bartholdi had designed a century before. Once again, teamwork between French and American workers got the job done. On July 4, 1986, another dedication celebration filled the skies with fireworks and cheers.

JOURNEY'S END

Visiting the Statue of Liberty is a journey in itself. First, people take a ferry to Liberty Island. Then they wait. More than 5 million people visit the statue each year. The statue always has a long waiting line.

Millions of visitors from around the world flock to view the New York area from the statue's crown.

Finally, visitors begin climbing the long stairway inside the pedestal. There are 192 steps just to get up to the statue's feet. Those who have trouble climbing can take an elevator for the first ten stories. But after that, it's stairs all the way to the top. Another 162 steps, and the weary travelers reach the statue's head. By this time, they have climbed 354 steps. As they stroll around the crown of the statue, most agree that

The dream of freedom in the United States never dies.

the view is well worth the effort.

One day, a very old lady boarded the Liberty ferry. For her, it was a dream come true. She had never forgotten the day she sailed into New York Harbor as a little girl eighty years before.

When she stepped off the ferry onto Liberty Island, her eyes filled with tears. She dropped to her knees and kissed the ground. For a second time, she gave thanks that she had come safely to her journey's end.

41

GLOSSARY

anniversary—a date people remember because an important event took place on that day

centennial—one-hundredth birthday

dedication—an opening ceremony

donations—gifts

enlightening—teaching; instructing

immigrants—people who come to another country to live

pedestal—a base that something stands on

persecution—cruel and unfair treatment

refugees—people driven from their country because of war, persecution, or natural disaster

DID YOU KNOW?

- Frédéric-Auguste Bartholdi used his mother's face as the model for the Statue of Liberty's face. His wife was the model for the arms.

- More than 35 million immigrants arrived in the Unites States between 1815 and 1930. The biggest year for immigration was 1907. More than 1,285,000 newcomers arrived that year.

- The Statue of Liberty is made of copper, and copper is the color of a new penny. So why does the Statue of Liberty look green? Because copper bonds with the oxygen in the air and forms copper oxide, which is greenish.

- The Statue of Liberty National Monument includes both the Statue of Liberty and Ellis Island.

- The Statue of Liberty's pedestal contains two museums.

IMPORTANT DATES

Timeline

1776	American colonists issue the Declaration of Independence.
1783	The American Revolution ends.
1871	Frédéric-Auguste Bartholdi tours the United States.
1884	The Statue of Liberty is completed.
1883–1885	The pedestal that the statue stands on is built.
1886	The statue is dedicated on October 28.
1986	The newly repaired statue has its 100th birthday celebration.

IMPORTANT PEOPLE

FRÉDÉRIC-AUGUSTE BARTHOLDI

(1834–1904), *French sculptor who designed the Statue of Liberty*

GROVER CLEVELAND

(1837–1908), *U.S. president who led the statue's dedication ceremony*

GUSTAVE EIFFEL

(1832–1923), *French engineer who designed the statue's framework*

RICHARD MORRIS HUNT

(1827–1895), *U.S. architect who designed the pedestal*

EMMA LAZARUS

(1849–1887), *poet whose poem "The New Colossus" was placed inside the pedestal*

WANT TO KNOW MORE?

At the Library

Bell, James B., and Richard I. Abrams. *In Search of Liberty: The Story of the Statue of Liberty and Ellis Island.* New York: Doubleday, 1984.

Miller, Natalie. *The Statue of Liberty.* Chicago: Childrens Press, 1992.

On the Web

Ellis Island

http://www.ellisisland.org

For complete information about Ellis Island, its history, and its museum

The Statue of Liberty Website

http://www.nps.gov/stli/mainmenu.htm

For complete information on the Statue of Liberty National Monument

Through the Mail

National Park Service

1849 C Street, N.W.

Washington, DC 20240

To get information about the Statue of Liberty National Monument

On the Road

Ellis Island Immigration Museum

Ellis Island

New York, NY 10004

212/363-3200

To learn about how immigrants were processed

Statue of Liberty National Monument

Liberty Island

New York, NY 10004

212/363-3200

To visit the Statue of Liberty

INDEX

About the Author

Ann Heinrichs was born in Fort Smith, Arkansas. She began playing the piano at age three and thought she would grow up to be a pianist. Instead, she became a writer. Now she has written more than thirty-five books for children and young adults. Ann Heinrichs lives in Chicago, Illinois.

By Herman Parish
Pictures by Lynn Sweat

Greenwillow Books, New York

Watercolor paints and a black pen were used for the full-color art.
The text type is Times.
Text copyright © 1999 by Herman S. Parish III
Illustrations copyright © 1999 by Lynn Sweat
All rights reserved. No part of this book may be reproduced or utilized in any form
or by any means, electronic or mechanical, including photocopying, recording, or by
any information storage and retrieval system, without permission in writing from
the Publisher, Greenwillow Books, a division of William Morrow & Company, Inc.,
1350 Avenue of the Americas, New York, NY 10019.   www.williammorrow.com
Printed in Singapore by Tien Wah Press
First Edition   10   9   8   7   6   5   4   3   2   1

Library of Congress Cataloging-in-Publication Data
Parish, Herman.
Amelia Bedelia 4 mayor / by Herman Parish ; illustrated by Lynn Sweat.
p.   cm.
Summary: A series of misunderstandings leads the literal-minded Amelia Bedelia to run for mayor.
ISBN 0-688-16721-7 (trade).   ISBN 0-688-16722-5 (lib. ed.)
[1. Politics, Practical—Fiction.   2. Humorous stories.]
I. Sweat, Lynn, ill.   II. Title.   III. Title: Amelia Bedelia four mayor.
PZ7.P219Amk   1999   [E]—dc21
98-46158   CIP   AC

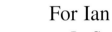

"That Mayor Thomas!" said Mr. Rogers.

"What's wrong, dear?" said Mrs. Rogers.

"Mayor Thomas is what's wrong,"
  said Mr. Rogers.

"The mayor promised to *cut* taxes.
  He never does what he says he will do."

"He is only human," said Mrs. Rogers.

"Besides, no one does exactly
  what you tell them to do."

"Here is your breakfast," said Amelia Bedelia.

"I hope you like chocolate frosting."

"What is this?" said Mr. Rogers.

"I said I wanted pancakes for breakfast."

"These *are* pan cakes," said Amelia Bedelia.

"I baked these cakes in a frying pan.

Do you want to blow out the candles?"

"They are fine," said Mrs. Rogers.

"I will teach you to make normal pancakes.

You just did what you were told."

"You always do," said Mr. Rogers.

"Why can't Mayor Thomas be like you?
 I wish you were the mayor."

"You do?" said Amelia Bedelia.

"Sure," said Mr. Rogers.

"You should run for the mayor's office."

"See you later," said Amelia Bedelia.

She dashed out of the kitchen.

"Where is she going?" said Mrs. Rogers.

"To City Hall!" said Mr. Rogers.

"She *is* running for the mayor's office!"

"I made it!" said Amelia Bedelia.

"Hold on," said the mayor's secretary.

"Mayor Thomas is with the press.
 He needs to iron out some things."

"I hate to iron," said Amelia Bedelia.

"I will bring him Mr. Rogers's shirts.
 The mayor can press them for me."

She burst into the press conference.

"Amelia Bedelia!" said Mayor Thomas.

"What brings you here?"

"My feet," said Amelia Bedelia.

"I was out running for your office."

"Running for office?" said a reporter.

"The mayor has very big shoes to fill."

"You are rude," said Amelia Bedelia.

"He can't help it if his feet are big."

"You are right," said a reporter.

"Big feet must run in his family."

"How awful," said Amelia Bedelia.

"Don't they ever get to walk?"

All the reporters laughed.

Mayor Thomas did not laugh.

"Ahhhh-CHOOO!" he sneezed.

"His nose runs, too," said a reporter.

"No," said Amelia Bedelia.

"His nose smells."

"I hope his feet don't,"
said the reporter.

"You *are* rude!" said the mayor.

"Amelia Bedelia," asked a reporter,

"what would you do

if you were in the mayor's shoes?"

"I would polish them," said Amelia Bedelia.

"They could use a good shine."

Mr. Rogers arrived out of breath.
"Amelia Bedelia, let's go home.
I was joking. You can't run for office."

"I just did," said Amelia Bedelia.
"I always do what folks say to do."
"That is a great promise to make,"
  said a reporter.

"I make promises, too," said the mayor.

"We know, we know," said Mr. Rogers.

"But if Amelia Bedelia were mayor . . ."

"You must be joking," said Mayor Thomas.

"Amelia Bedelia can't be the mayor."

"I would vote for her," said a reporter.

"We need some change."

"Here's 43 cents," said Amelia Bedelia.

"That's all the change I've got."

"Wait a minute," said the mayor.

"I want to put in my two cents."

"How nice," said Amelia Bedelia.

"That makes 45 cents."

"No, no, no," said the mayor.

"'My two cents' means 'my opinion.'
I don't really have two cents."

"You don't?" said Amelia Bedelia.

"Then you should get some cents."

"Mayor Thomas doesn't have any sense?"
asked a reporter.

"Is that what you just said?"

"No, *he* said that," said Amelia Bedelia.

"I did not!" said the mayor.

"I said I don't have two *pennies*."

"Me neither," said Mr. Rogers.

"I hope Mayor Bedelia cuts taxes."

"*Mayor* Bedelia!" yelled Mayor Thomas.

"She couldn't even be the dog catcher!"

"Yes, I could!" said Amelia Bedelia.

"Take back what you just said!"

"I will not!" said the mayor.

"Run for mayor," said a reporter.

"Throw your hat in the ring."

"What ring?" said Amelia Bedelia.

The mayor's telephone rang.

RING
RING

MAYOR

Amelia Bedelia took off her hat.

She threw it across the room.

Her hat landed on top of the phone.

"How's that?" said Amelia Bedelia.

"I threw my hat *on* the ring.

Now I can run for mayor."

Amelia Bedelia crouched down.
"On your mark, get set, GO!"
"Hooray!" shouted everyone—
everyone except Mayor Thomas.

The race for mayor was on.

Amelia Bedelia

and Mayor Thomas

ran all over town

to talk with the voters.

People began to care more about their town,
about each other, and their future.

Mr. Rogers gave Amelia Bedelia

lots of help and plenty of good advice.

"Yikes!" said Mr. Rogers.

"Gotcha," said Amelia Bedelia.

"Here's that pole you told me to get."

"Not a fishing pole," said Mr. Rogers.

"What you need is a *voting poll*.

It tells how voters plan to cast their votes."

"Cast votes?" asked Amelia Bedelia.

"Sounds like fishing to me."

"Most voters are sitting on the fence,"
 said Mr. Rogers.
"And you know what that means."
"Sore bottoms," said Amelia Bedelia.

"*Not* sore bottoms," said Mr. Rogers.
"It means people haven't made up their minds.
 This election isn't sewn up yet."

"Hold my pole," said Amelia Bedelia.

"I'll go get a needle and thread.

I will sew it up."

"Forget about sewing and fishing,"

said Mr. Rogers.

"Go out and get some more votes."

Amelia Bedelia walked to town.

A crowd was at the new bridge.

"When I cut this ribbon," said the mayor,
"this brand-new bridge will be open!"
Amelia Bedelia stepped in front of him.
She cut that red ribbon before he did.

SNIP!

"What have you done!" said the mayor.

"Cut that red tape," said Amelia Bedelia.

"Everyone says I should get rid of red tape."

"This is an outrage!" said the mayor.

"You wrecked my photo opportunity."

"Are you having your picture taken?"
said Amelia Bedelia.

"Then you really should smile!"

"That does it!" shouted the mayor.

"I challenge you to a debate!
  People will know where I stand."

"I can tell them where you are standing,"
  said Amelia Bedelia.

"On my foot! Owwwwwie!"

On the day of the debate,

the town square was packed.

"Now, let's welcome the mayor

and Amelia Bedelia!" said the announcer.

Everyone clapped and cheered.

"I am nervous," said Amelia Bedelia.

"Just be yourself," said Mrs. Rogers.

"I always am," said Amelia Bedelia.

"Who else would I be?"

Mr. and Mrs. Rogers each gave her a big hug.

The mayor and Amelia Bedelia
argued for hours.
"I will fill in all the potholes,"
said Mayor Thomas.
"Me, too," said Amelia Bedelia.
"You can't cook in pots with holes."
"That's silly," said the mayor.

"It sure is," said Amelia Bedelia.

"All the food falls out."

"That's right!" yelled the crowd.

"I will reduce the school tax,"
 said Mayor Thomas.

"And I won't," said Amelia Bedelia.

"Our schools need more tacks.
 Especially thumbtacks."

"You tell him!" shouted the crowd.

"My goodness!" said Mrs. Rogers.

"They are fighting like cats and dogs."

HI-SSST! BOW-WOW-WOW!

A big dog chased a cat across the stage.

Mayor Thomas rescued the cat,
Amelia Bedelia grabbed the dog.
"Good job!" said Mayor Thomas.

"You mean that?" said Amelia Bedelia.

"I sure do," said Mayor Thomas.

"You proved that you can be the dog catcher.
I take back what I said. I apologize to you."

"I accept your apology," said Amelia Bedelia.

"And now I can stop running for mayor."

"No! Don't quit!" shouted the crowd.

"Listen to me," said Amelia Bedelia.

"I said I would run for mayor *unless*

   Mayor Thomas took back what he said.

   He took it back.

   So now I don't have to run any more."

No one moved or made a sound.

"I admire you," said the mayor.

"You know how to keep a promise."

He began to clap for Amelia Bedelia.

Then the whole crowd joined in.

"Good news," said Mr. Rogers.

"The mayor kept his promise."

"See there," said Mrs. Rogers.

"You *can* teach an old dog new tricks."

"I don't have time," said Amelia Bedelia.

"And I am *not* catching any more dogs.

I am going to the White house."

"The White House!" said Mr. Rogers.

"You are going to Washington?"

"Of course not," said Amelia Bedelia.

"I borrowed a book from Mrs. White.

She said to leave it at her house."

WHEW!

"Whew!" said Mr. Rogers.

"I thought you were running for president!"

"I will do whatever you say,"

  said Amelia Bedelia.

  Mr. Rogers did not say one more word . . .

even when he got his French toast.